Effective Decision-Making

Steven M. Bragg

AccountingTools®

ISBN 978-1-64221-232-7

For more information about AccountingTools® products, visit our Web site at www.accountingtools.com.

Table of Contents

About the Author

Steven Bragg, CPA, has been the chief financial officer or controller of four companies, as well as a consulting manager at Ernst & Young. He received a master's degree in finance from Bentley College, an MBA from Babson College, and a Bachelor's degree in Economics from the University of Maine. He has been a two-time president of the Colorado Mountain Club, and is an avid alpine skier, mountain biker, and certified master diver. Mr. Bragg resides in Centennial, Colorado. He has written more than 300 books and courses, including *New Controller Guidebook*, *GAAP Guidebook*, and *Payroll Management*.

Steven maintains the accountingtools.com web site, which contains continuing professional education courses, the Accounting Best Practices podcast, and thousands of articles on accounting subjects.

Buy Additional AccountingTools Courses

AccountingTools offers more than 1,500 hours of CPE courses, with concentrations in accounting, auditing, finance, taxation, and ethics. Related courses that you might like include:

- Business Strategy
- Effective Leadership
- Effective Negotiation
- New Manager Guidebook

Go to accountingtools.com/cpe to view these additional courses.

AccountingTools®

Effective Decision-Making

Introduction

Your company's finances are stretched at the moment, but your business development team has spotted a choice acquisition opportunity where the target company's products would nicely complement your product line. Or, your vice president of engineering wants to make a large investment in automation on a product line, but it is currently losing money. What is your process for making these types of decisions?

Problems like this arise every day, covering a range of topics from hiring job candidates to deciding upon which project proposals to fund. Making the best decisions is not easy, because you never have enough time to devote to a full appraisal of the options, the supporting data may be weak, you have unacknowledged biases, and so forth. There are ways to improve your approach to making decisions when the choices are not clear. In the following pages, we cover a number of concepts that clarify how to make decisions in the most effective manner possible.

Why Decision-Making is So Hard

Before we get into solutions, why is decision-making so hard? The trouble is the stew of conflicting issues that can muddy the decision-making waters. In the following examples, we note many of the problems that can arise:

- *Anchoring*. Decisions tend to be minor extensions of a baseline situation, because the decision-maker unconsciously creates boundaries around the range of possible decisions based on the current situation. For example, when a landlord proposes a certain price per square foot on a lease renewal, the tenant tends to bargain only a short distance away from what the landlord has proposed, rather than being more aggressive. Or, a prospective publisher offers an author a royalty rate of 10%, from which the author tries to negotiate another 1% boost in the rate – rather than considering the 50% rate associated with self-publishing. Anchoring tends to reduce the span of possible decision outcomes.
- *Data problems*. The data on which a decision is based are conflicting or inadequate. For example, the decision is whether to develop a product for an entirely new product niche, but it is impossible to determine the size of this market; it could be so small that no units are sold, or it could be large enough to drive much of the company's growth.
- *Overconfidence*. People think that they can devise estimates of future outcomes within a narrow range. In reality, outcomes tend to fall well outside of these estimated outcomes. People either miss major opportunities (because their forecast was too low) or expose themselves to substantial risks (because their forecast was too high).

- *Risks*. Different risks may be associated with different decision options, and it is not clear how likely those risks are to occur, or the costs associated with each one. For example, a manager is trying to decide whether her company should produce jogger baby carriages, but does not know what the cost of a lawsuit might be if the product were to fail.
- *Time pressure*. One of the most common issues is the need to make a decision right now – usually due to competitive pressures. When you are under time pressure, it is nearly impossible to collect sufficient data or review the available options. For example, the competitor of an electric car company has just rolled out a new model that doubles the driving range of its previous model. If the company president does not make a public announcement right away to stem the flow of orders to the competitor, the business will start to lose sales. What should he include in the announcement?
- *Emotion*. The introduction of emotions into decision-making can skew the outcome, and usually away from the optimal decision. The fear of failure can shift a decision into a more conservative outcome, while the eagerness to prove yourself could shift a decision too far in the opposite direction. For example, the CEO of a company that has just gone public decides to jump aggressively into a new market, mostly because he is afraid of the response from institutional investors if he does not.
- *Biases*. Decisions tend to be skewed because of inherent biases, which block you from even considering new options. For example, a person only looks at data that confirm his opinion that sales are declining in the southeast region, and so decides to fund a massive advertising campaign in that region.
- *Shortcuts*. Given the time constraints that many people are under, they frequently copy decisions they have made in the past – just to avoid the data collection and analysis steps that they would normally have to walk through. For example, why would a purchasing manager review a new supplier when the company has been buying from the existing one for ten years?
- *Sunk costs*. When a large amount of money has already been poured into a project, there is a strong tendency to keep doing so – even when it becomes apparent that the original expectations for the project will not be met. For example, a government has spent massive amounts constructing a series of bridges from the mainland to a distant set of islands – but now the population of the islands is declining. Do you abandon the project or keep pouring money into it?
- *Historical weighting*. There is a strong tendency to give an inordinate amount of weight to historical data in making projections. The problem is that doing so ignores other factors, which can result in poor decisions, usually to continue investing in existing product lines. For example, a manager decides to make a major investment in the further development of a diesel engine, based on historical demand for this product – despite the actions of multiple governments to ban these engines within the next decade.

What makes the preceding issues dangerous is that they tend to be invisible. When a bad decision is made, it is quite likely that the decision-maker fell afoul of one or more of these traps and never realized it. For example, one might never question whether the underlying data was correct, or whether it might be possible to delay making a decision in order to ponder it further. In short, these issues tend to operate in the background, and never bubble up into one's conscious decision-making processes.

When you familiarize yourself with these issues, it is easier to recognize them as part of the decision-making process, yielding better decisions.

EXAMPLE

Joe Fitzpatrick, the vice president of distribution for International Baubles, needs a new warehouse management system for the 100,000+ baubles that his company distributes around the world. Unfortunately, he is deeply appreciative of a well-cut suit, which is why he decides to buy the warehouse management software sold by an extremely well-dressed salesman. He then calls a few of his buddies who confirm that the software has worked well for them (though their businesses are different). Over time, Joe realizes that he needs to keep buying more software modules to address the needs of his distribution operation, resulting in spiraling costs that are well beyond his original budget.

In this case, Joe's decision-making is slanted by his bias towards well-dressed people, followed by his use of confirmation bias, followed by his falling into the sunk cost trap. In short, a series of flaws result in a bad decision.

Examples of Difficult Decisions

The commentary in this book is focused on clarifying how to resolve the more difficult decisions. Here are several examples of the topics to which these decision-making tools could be applied:

- *Product decisions*. Should you expand the existing product line or develop a product in an entirely new market? The first option is safer, since there is an established customer base that will buy it, but the second option will introduce the company to an entirely new set of customers.
- *New hires*. Should you hire an experienced person to take over a position who is likely to retire in the next five years, or hire an inexperienced youngster with lots of new ideas? The first option brings stability to the position, while the section option might result in a number of best practices being implemented within the department.
- *Complex software installations*. You are interested in installing a company-wide enterprise resource planning system, but realize that the installation will be lengthy, fraught with departmental conflicts, and expensive. Should you proceed, or allow each department to install its own systems instead?
- *Outsourcing*. Should you move some company functions to a third party, such as customer service or manufacturing? This is an especially difficult decision when doing so reduces the flexibility of the organization, removes people with

essential skills, and/or ties the company into a long-term contract. These issues must be balanced against a reduction in costs and capital investments.

- *Acquisitions.* Among the most difficult of all decisions is the acquisition. Should you buy another company or not? Doing so brings in the acquiree's intellectual property, skilled staff, and existing product line, but also carries the major risks of employee and customer departures, a poor integration process, and cash flows that do not justify the acquisition price.

Step 1: Determine Who Makes the Decision

The first step in making a decision is deciding who is responsible for it. This is a particular concern with larger decisions, such as where to site a new company facility or which product to develop. For example, the marketing department might think that it has the final say on whether a new product should be released, which may conflict with the managers of the sales, engineering, and production departments. When this is the case, decisions are routinely revisited and revised, which delays the final decision – if it is ever made at all.

To avoid these problems, senior management should develop a list of who will make which decisions. For example, the sales manager decides which new markets to enter, while the marketing manager has the final say on new product features, and the engineering manager decides whether a product recall is necessary. This list should only be developed for major decisions; the many more decisions that fall entirely within the boundaries of a single functional area should be the sole responsibility of the manager of that area.

The determination of who decides is not actually quite that simple. It may be necessary for the designated decision-maker to gain input from specific parties. For example, if the marketing manager has the final say on new product features, it would be entirely reasonable to require the input of the engineering manager (who has to design it) and the production manager (who has to manufacture it), as well as the purchasing manager (who has to source the parts for it).

Step 2: Generate Options

The next step in the decision-making process is to generate options from which a final decision can be made, as noted in the following sub-sections.

Conduct a Root Cause Analysis

Before generating options for an eventual decision, it might make sense to ensure that the underlying problem has been found. This can be done with *root cause analysis*, which is the process of looking for the reasons why a problem is occurring. By correcting the underlying root causes of problems, their incidence can be greatly reduced or eliminated. Root cause analysis tends to uncover issues related to the failure of materials, an error by a person, or an organizational issue (such as an incorrect work instruction, procedure, or form).

Root cause analysis can be used in a variety of areas. For example, it can be used to uncover the reasons for incorrect billings, product failures, and vehicle accidents on a particular stretch of road. It is most heavily applied to the resolution of product failure issues, but can be readily adapted to the analysis of failures in company processes.

This analysis may require a considerable amount of detailed investigation, not only to find a root cause, but also to generate several possible solutions that will correct it. The solution selected will usually be the simplest or least expensive alternative available, and one that does not trigger a new root cause that leads to a new problem or reinforces an old one.

EXAMPLE

The Magic Stroller Company finds that there is a high return rate by customers for its baby stroller product, because there are repeated instances where the wheels fall off. After conducting a root cause analysis, the firm's engineering manager finds that the nut used to tighten the wheels onto the axles has the wrong specifications, which it corrects on the next purchase of nuts from a supplier. As a result, the company finds that product returns are reduced, but do not go away, due to the same complaint. Additional root cause analysis finds that the axle onto which the nut is tightened can break off, due to metal fatigue. As a result, the purchasing department buys the axle component with more stringent specifications, after which the returns issue is eliminated.

Frame the Question

What is the question that you are trying to solve? This seems like an elementary question, and yet it can be the source of endless decision-making problems if it is not framed properly. In many cases, it locks in the decision-maker on the status quo, and so only allows for modest improvements.

EXAMPLE

A company wants to reduce its shipping costs. The manager in charge of the issues frames the question as how to negotiate a better package rate with the United States Postal Service. This framing limits the solution to working with the current provider.

A more broad-based framing, such as to reduce shipping costs, allows for a broader range of solutions, including accepting bids from other shippers and setting up an in-house package delivery service.

If the question was framed by someone else, a good way to improve upon it is to re-frame it yourself. Better yet, re-frame it several ways, to see if any particular framing opens up a broader range of opportunities for solutions.

EXAMPLE

The students at a local middle school are earning below-average grades. A possible framing of this problem is to determine the class configuration that will result in the highest grades – except that doing so only addresses the configuration of the classroom. Yet another option is to frame the problem as identifying those students whose grades are the lowest, on the theory that bringing the grades of this group up will help the entire school. A third option is to frame the question as determining whether particular teachers are not improving the scores of students – which might lead to the replacement of some teachers.

Generate *Lots* of Options

Decision-making is greatly improved when you have a broad range of options from which to select. Otherwise, a decision is essentially a binary call – whether to go with a single alternative or do nothing at all. Doing so rarely results in the optimal outcome.

EXAMPLE

Phil Hudson is the owner of Hudson Motor Parts, which distributes automobile parts to do-it-yourself customers by mail. The company has just entered the Canadian market, and sales are well below expectations. Phil calls a meeting of the senior management team to discuss the issue. He suggests that advertising by a mailed catalog may no longer be the best way to go, at which point a number of people follow up on this thought, concentrating the attention of everyone on the catalog situation.

The problem is that no additional ideas are being explored, such as the use of overnight deliveries, an Internet store, and the use of retail stores in selected locations. Because Phil immediately brought up the catalog, everyone followed his lead, leaving vast swathes of possibilities completely untouched.

One person may have a hard time coming up with more than a couple of options, so this is a good time to employ brainstorming to collect ideas from more people. *Brainstorming* is a process used to generate ideas by engaging in an open group discussion. Each person in the group is encouraged to come up with as many ideas as possible, no matter how outlandish they may initially appear to be. A critique of the resulting ideas is only allowed after the initial idea generation phase has been completed. By barring any initial negative feedback on suggestions, people feel less inclined to keep ideas to themselves. This technique is frequently used to derive "out of the box" alternatives to improve processes and products.

> **Tip:** When setting up a brainstorming meeting, do not just invite the people currently involved with the issue – also bring in outsiders and newer employees. These additions may have a different perspective on the issues that result in some of the best ideas; the reason is that they have not been locked into the traditional way of thinking about the problem, and have no investment in the status quo.

In many cases, what might initially be considered outlier ideas turn out to be the best decision alternatives.

Ask "Stupid" Questions

Sometimes, the most profound decision outcomes stem from a "stupid" question. These questions usually come from junior people who have not been with the company long enough to be trained in "how things are done around here," and are willing to throw out questions so "stupid" that they would be dismissed out of hand by more senior people. These questions typically revolve around assumptions that everyone else feels are set in concrete, even though this is not necessarily the case.

Assumptions are an especially rich target for such questioning, because they are frequently essential to the outcome of a decision, and yet are rarely questioned. The usual situation is that a business has been operating under a small number of key assumptions for a long time, and assumes that they will not change – until they do.

EXAMPLE

A construction company builds homes in the American southwest. It bases its planning for new home construction on a small number of assumptions, which are that mortgage rates will remain low for the foreseeable future, that the existing economic conditions remain about the same (thereby supporting roughly the current level of customer demand) and that the cost of building materials will remain the same.

While it is entirely possible that one or even two of these assumptions will remain reasonable for the next decade, it is not likely to be the case for all three. Consequently, a periodic re-examination of these assumptions is warranted.

As long as you are actually willing to consider these questions, it is entirely possible that a golden nugget of an idea may be hiding inside them. These are the "outside the box" concepts that can occasionally provide a breakthrough outcome. The problem is that these questions can put more experienced people on the defensive, and so they tend to reject them at once, rather than spending the time to consider whether the questioner actually has a good point.

> **Tip:** It is especially important to ask "stupid" questions in situations where the competitive environment is changing fast. At these times, a business might need to rethink its approach to many aspects of its sales, marketing, operations, and so forth several times a year.

Step 3: Evaluate Alternatives

The options created in the preceding step can be reviewed in quite a few ways to gain insights into which one might be the best alternative – as noted in the following subsections.

Ensure that Stakeholders are Included

One of the most concerning issues that can arise is after a decision has been made, when some parties claim that they were not consulted, and want to re-open the decision-making process. The best way to deal with this scenario is to keep it from happening. This means drawing up a list of every stakeholder in the process (that is, those who will be affected by it) and obtain their opinions. It can make sense to regularly return to this group with your latest findings and possible alternatives; doing so gives them a sense of inclusion in the process, and allows them to provide additional input. In cases where people will be deeply impacted by the outcome, consider including them on the team that is involved in formulating it.

Tip: The trick to including stakeholders in the process is deciding when to keep adding more of them. Having a massive group of stakeholders to consult with is unwieldy. A good cutoff point is to only include those parties whose performance will be *significantly* impacted by the decision.

Explain Your Decision-Making Process

When other people will be impacted by your decision, it makes sense to explain to them your decision-making process up front. Once they understand that the process is intended to be fair, they are more likely to be supportive of your ultimate decision. It is especially important to take this step when it is likely that the final outcome will not provide an equitable impact for all parties concerned. In most cases, someone will be impacted negatively, so they need to understand why.

Explaining the decision-making process is especially important when those affected will be involved in the eventual implementation of the alternative selected. Having them pulling together on the back end of the decision is critical for achieving a successful outcome.

EXAMPLE

The production department has persistently been shipping goods that contain quality problems, all of which can be traced back to that department. The vice president of production meets with the entire department to discuss how he will handle the situation. This will involve an analysis of all types of quality issues found, to determine exactly which processes are causing the problems. Once root causes have been found, he will make changes in the department that are focused on eliminating the highest-volume quality problems first. He notes that this may involve the use of automation, which could result in the loss of some jobs.

Review the Impact on Goals

Itemize any existing company goals that may be impacted by the decision, and consider *how* they will be impacted. Doing so in advance makes it difficult to rationalize your thinking after the fact. Instead, if you know up-front that a particular decision will have a negative impact on a company goal, you will be less likely to select that option.

Taking this approach also creates some emotional distance from a decision option. You might *really* want to go with a particular choice, but the mere process of reviewing likely outcomes can temper that initial enthusiasm, resulting in a better-reasoned outcome. In addition, taking the time to think through outcomes provides a gap in time in which your emotions can dissipate – again resulting in a better outcome.

Evaluate the Status Quo

When evaluating alternatives, also evaluate the status quo – that is, doing nothing at all. To keep from automatically selecting the status quo, consider every element of the current situation that keeps you from achieving your goals.

When your initial review of the situation appears to indicate that the only alternative is the status quo, conduct a search for other options. This may involve asking others for their opinions. If any alternatives are found, compare them to the status quo, feature by feature, to see if there are any serious rivals worth considering. In addition, consider just how difficult it would be to switch away from the status quo, noting both the time and cost required. In many cases, these steps will help to clarify that it is not all that difficult to switch to a different option.

Evaluate Missing Information

Review each decision alternative and see if there is any information missing that could impact your decision. Perhaps pricing information is missing, or historical data about the performance of a particular manufacturing process. If so, decide whether it makes sense to delay making a decision until the information can be obtained.

EXAMPLE

A company president is pondering whether to relocate her manufacturing facility to a rural area where labor rates are lower. As part of the evaluation process, she makes a list of the information she does not know about this location – including the availability of utilities, the risk of flooding, the impact on the price of her general insurance policy, and whether delivery trucks will have reliable access to it. She wants to learn more about each of these topics before making a decision.

Separate Facts from Estimates

Some of the data being used as the basis for a decision have impeccable sources, while other data may be more problematic. When you are uncertain of data sources, consider spending time early in the evaluation process digging into this issue. In particular, data that are merely estimates should be identified as such, and so should be treated with more suspicion than higher-grade data, such as audited financial reports.

The quality of data is a particular concern when evaluating proposals for capital investments, where much of the data involves forecasts. In these cases, be aware of the possibility that the person presenting the proposal might have adjusted the underlying forecasts in order to arrive at a net present value for the project that is sure to be approved. When you suspect that this may be the case, dig into the key assumptions of the proposal with a higher degree of rigor.

Look for Discrepancies

It is all too common for major decisions to be made based on misleading or faulty information. To see if this is the case, question everyone providing data to determine where they obtained it. Also, look for discrepancies between different data sets; when there are significant variances, *something* is wrong, and certainly requires further investigation.

Evaluate Sunk Costs

In cases where large amounts of time and effort have been sunk into previous investment decisions, formally evaluate the investment on a go-forward basis. Does it still make sense? This is the *sunk cost* trap, where funds have been spent and cannot be recovered, and yet more funds are spent in order to justify the original decision.

EXAMPLE

A CFO hired a controller two years ago who has a number of personal relations issues. Rather than admitting his mistake, the CFO hires a coach for the controller, who has provided a great deal of expensive support for many months. This is a sunk cost. The CFO may be having trouble admitting that he originally made a bad hiring decision, and so keeps pouring coaching fees into the original investment when a clean break is the better solution.

Tip: In cases where the original manager is still pouring funds into an investment that is clearly not working out, the best solution may be to shift responsibility for it to a different person. The replacement manager has no history with the investment, and so is better able to cut it, if necessary.

When it appears that a business is continually getting caught in the sunk cost trap, the reason for it may be a company policy that imposes severe penalties when a project fails. To keep from incurring these penalties, managers keep allocating funds to projects that should have been shut down long ago. To avoid this trap, senior managers need to address how they deal with failed projects.

Tip: When evaluating an investment for which there are significant sunk costs, discuss the matter with someone who was not involved in the original decision, and who can therefore offer an unbiased view of the situation.

Evaluate Bottlenecks

Bottlenecks are the bane of many decisions. You might think that you have a great solution to a problem, but then it turns out that the one person who can help you implement it is away on sabbatical for six months. Because of this concern, it makes sense to review each decision option in terms of any possible bottlenecks, to evaluate their impact. There are a number of possible bottlenecks to consider, such as the availability of funding, senior management approval, equipment, facilities, and qualified personnel.

In some cases, there may initially appear to be enough resources, but only *just* enough, so that any incident triggers a bottleneck after a decision has been made, which impedes implementation. For example, a vice president can just barely scrape together enough funding for a new automated inventory retrieval system in the warehouse, but then a major hardware failure requires the purchase of new computer equipment, which leaves a shortfall to fund the retrieval system. It can be useful to evaluate all situations like this, where resources are sufficient but only a modest failure could negatively impact the decision.

EXAMPLE

Eve has a choice of hiring a company to install office cubicles for her in a new company location, with all services included. Or, she can separately hire contractors for each phase of the work for half the price. She opts for the second alternative, and arranges to have wiring completed, phone lines installed, and cubicles delivered and assembled. Only then does she realize that the company requires shielded network cabling for every computer in the cubicles, because the company is certified by the government to handle top-secret information – which cannot be transmitted over wi-fi. Due to the special nature of this cabling, it will be two weeks before the installation can be completed. Murphy's Law strikes again, where the wiring availability creates a bottleneck.

Investigate Motivations

When someone is bringing you a proposal, a reasonable question to ask is the nature of their motivation for doing so. Whether they realize it or not, it is entirely possible that they are driven more by self-interest than the good of the company. For example, when you receive a suggestion from a company manager to acquire another business, a reasonable question to ask is whether that manager expects to run it. Or, if the sales manager proposes a change in the sales commission structure, you might investigate how that change will impact her own income. These motivations may be caused by the usual inducement of more personal income, but might also be driven by a desire to gain more power within the company or burnish one's resume.

Investigate the Love Effect

Though the title of this sub-section is odd, the point is real enough. When people fall in love with a particular decision option, they tend to discount or ignore any problems associated with it. For example, if the company president has always wanted to acquire a key competitor and now has the chance to do so, she is more likely to ignore a number of problems, such as its stale profits, declining customer base, and product line that is in need of an update. These can be significant concerns, especially when the love effect causes a business to invest far more in a decision option than a more clear-eyed person would pay. In short, when there is an emotional aspect to a decision, be especially thorough about investigating its pluses and minuses.

Investigate Dissenting Opinions

When a team of subordinates brings you a proposal, ask whether it was a unanimous decision to do so. Or did the group leader impose the decision on everyone else? By delving into this question, you may find that some team members have reservations about the proposal, and may even have devised quite detailed reports concerning their issues. If so, this constitutes an excellent source of information that can be used in your decision analysis.

> **Tip:** When there is no sign of dissenting opinions among the team, this can be a cause for concern, since it may be an indicator of *groupthink*, where the need for conformity results in a dysfunctional decision-making outcome.

Evaluate Time to Completion

As we noted in a preceding example, Murphy's Law[1] can strike at any time. To minimize this risk, it can make sense to review decision options in terms of how much time will pass before they can be completed. When the duration is expected to be long, it is more likely that unforeseen problems will arise, such as regulatory changes, a decline in executive support, and the loss of resources. Conversely, when one decision option can be implemented quickly, you might be more inclined to take it.

EXAMPLE

Harry has the choice of paying more money to a tried-and-true contractor to complete the installation of a production line in one month for a 20% premium, or paying a similarly-qualified contractor to complete the job within a time frame that is two months longer. Is the 20% premium worth the reduction in risk associated with the quicker completion date?

Evaluate the Risk of Failure

Some alternatives have a much higher risk of failure than others. This concept is usually associated with bleeding-edge technological solutions that could fail catastrophically, but the concept can be applied in other ways. For example, what is the risk that entering into a new trading relationship with a foreign supplier will fail due to the imposition of tariffs? There may be a high risk of failure in conducting underwater

---

[1] Murphy's Law is the adage that anything that can go wrong, will go wrong.

tours of a local reef with a submersible, because it leaks. Or, there is the risk that a production facility in a small third-world country will be expropriated by the government. Thus, the risk of failure can crop up in association with almost any decision, and especially ones that are unusually complex and involve large investments.

Giving more consideration to the risk of failure does not necessarily mean that you always select the alternatives for which the associated risks are the lowest. However, it *does* mean that you have to analyze the risk of failure and how this risk can be mitigated – which may alter the actions incorporated into a decision (see the next example).

EXAMPLE

A car company is exploring whether a new technology, molecular batteries, can be used to power its vehicles. Molecular batteries promise to be much smaller than normal battery packs, and so will reduce the weight of its vehicles and also call for a complete redesign of its cars, so that they retain the firm's racing car driving characteristics.

The risk that the batteries will not work is massive, but the firm wants to be on the leading edge of this technology. Accordingly, it hedges its bet by only investing in the development of a molecular battery-powered car for its racing team, so that the investment is highly restricted. If the batteries are proven to work on the racing circuit, then the company will consider rolling them out in a later line of cars.

Evaluate the Risk of Loss

This is not the same as the preceding topic of evaluating the risk of failure. The question is, how much money could you lose? For example, what kind of monetary losses could the company pay out if a customer were to be killed or injured by its products? Will the decision to open a new production facility open up the company to environmental damages claims due to groundwater contamination? By opening a subsidiary in another country with stringent labor laws, might the firm be prevented from closing down its facilities for an extended period of time? By selling flood insurance in areas near the Mississippi River, is an insurer taking on an excessively high risk of loss on water damage claims? In other words, the evaluation of losses is really a search for inordinately large losses that are tied to certain decision outcomes. Finding loss issues of this magnitude does not necessarily block the associated alternatives from being selected, but you must be aware of the losses when making a decision.

Consider the Reactions of Competitors

Nearly all of the considerations noted in this book are internal to the business. But in some cases, a decision will have an impact on competitors, such as a change in one's pricing or product features that will impact the sales of other industry players. When this is the case, consider what their reactions might be, as well as the timing of those reactions. For example, a competitor who sees your business enacting a price cut will likely do the same in order to preserve its market share. Similarly, a move to offer free shipping may be replicated throughout the industry. There may be a delay in these reactions, especially when your business is a niche player. The offerings of smaller companies may be overlooked by their larger competitors.

Evaluate Ethical Ramifications

There may be ethical considerations associated with some decision options. For example, in the face of declining sales, should a company conduct a mass layoff or impose reduced work hours for everyone in order to maintain full employment? Decisions that may make sense from a profitability perspective may make less sense when viewed from the perspective of the community in which the firm operates, or its customers or suppliers.

EXAMPLE

The chief executive officers of two mining companies played a round of golf. During the round, one of the CEOs mentioned the size of his IT department, which was quite small. The CEO had figured out how to get by on quite a small amount of IT services. Following the round, the other CEO went back to the office and laid off all but one of his IT staff. Was this right from an ethical perspective? One might argue that the livelihoods of the IT personnel should be balanced against increased profits. [Note: This event actually happened]

A good way to analyze a decision is to put yourself in the shoes of every person who will be impacted by your decision. If the impact would be negative, how would you feel in their place? How would you want to be treated? What would you consider to be fair treatment?

EXAMPLE

A pandemic strikes, and a website that matches up travelers with hotel rooms finds that its site traffic (and commissions) drop by 90%. It clearly cannot maintain its current cost structure, and there will certainly need to be layoffs, since there is no hard date by which the pandemic will end. The company recently went public, and has lots of cash in the bank.

After considerable deliberation, the company decides to lay off half of its employees, giving each of them six months of severance pay and fully-paid medical insurance for a year. While this approach might seem expensive, it also generates massive goodwill in the community, and very likely a group of former employees who would jump at the chance to work for the firm again.

Seek Out Alternative Viewpoints

When sorting through the various decision options, find someone who has taken an approach that differs from the direction in which you are currently headed. Doing so exposes you to a different outcome, and allows for an examination of how that outcome and its ramifications differ from your current direction. This approach is a good way to avoid *confirmation bias*, where the decision-maker only seeks out others who have the same opinions.

EXAMPLE

The CEO of a clothing retailer is concerned that ongoing trade wars will result in tariffs being imposed on goods shipped in from other countries. He calls the CEOs of several other companies who also source goods overseas, and hears the same opinion from them. The result, predictably, is to bring production back to locations within the country.

If he had sought out other CEOs who were going against the crowd and keeping their production overseas, he might have noted an alternative, which is to move production to countries that are least likely to get into trade spats with the United States. Doing so would allow the firm to maintain a lower cost structure than would be the case if production were brought back in-country.

> **Tip:** Question whether you are treating confirming information with the same rigor that you are treating other information. It is quite possible that you are being too lenient with confirming data.

Ponder Extreme Outcomes

Be sure to spend time pondering whether the highest-possible and lowest-possible estimates really represent the outer boundaries of what might happen. This means gaining an understanding of what events might cause these extreme outcomes to occur (such as a pandemic). People tend to focus too much on outcomes that are not too far away from the current activity level, and do not consider the impact of major changes.

EXAMPLE

Garuda Mining, which operates several coal mines, is estimating a 2% decline in sales per year for the next decade. Its president ponders the impact of legislation curtailing the use of coal in the regions his firm services, and concludes that a maximum possible decline of 8% per year is possible, if not likely.

EXAMPLE

A manufacturer of food carts for sports venues invests millions in new design and production capabilities, based on a generous estimated increase in sales. An analysis by a cautious controller determines that such an increase is greater than the entire current market for food carts – resulting in a sharp decline in planned increases in sales.

Assign a Devil's Advocate

Though few people like to play the role, it can be useful to assign someone the position of devil's advocate, always challenging the assumptions of everyone else in the decision-making group. This conversation can include a discussion of any issues that might cause a proposal to fail.

The reason why a devil's advocate is so useful is that it creates tension; when tension is present, people are more likely to scrutinize options and explore alternatives in more detail, which can lead to a broader range of possible options. In short, making things harder fosters more innovative thinking.

It can be quite useful for the manager making the decision to take this role, so that no one else in the group knows which way she is leaning; this triggers a livelier debate.

> **Tip:** Rotate the devil's advocate role among your advisors. Anyone who is weak in the role may be too accustomed to being a "yes man," in which case it is time to find a different advisor.

Revisit Abandoned Ideas

Before settling upon your final choice, conduct a review of ideas that have already been abandoned. Since more information may have been compiled since then, and your perspective may have changed, it is possible that one of these ideas might actually be better than the options considered to be the final choices.

View All Options Together

It is more productive to view all possible options together, rather than in sequence. This approach makes it easier to conduct a thorough comparison of options. When options are viewed sequentially, you are more likely to dismiss some options at once, so that the stack of possibilities is winnowed down too soon. It is especially useful to take this approach when there are many variables to sort through.

EXAMPLE

The accounting department of a manufacturing company is searching for a new software package. The reviewers want to optimize a range of functions, including task automation features, availability on widely distributed platforms, and electronic payment features. No software package contains everything on the department's wish list. Following the advice of a decision-making consultant, the review team assembles the features of all software packages being reviewed into a single spreadsheet, so that it can compare and contrast the various features.

When comparing alternatives, it can make sense to assemble the key decision points in a table. Doing so is time-consuming, and so will probably be limited to only the larger decisions. For example, the controller of a mid-sized publicly-held manufacturing company with subsidiaries in several Spanish-speaking countries is in desperate need of an assistant controller. She has been unable to find the perfect candidate, but three applicants possess a mix of the skills she needs. She creates the following table to evaluate her choices.

Sample Comparison Table

	Andy	Bob	Carla
Largest business in a similar role	$120 million	$500 million	$90 million
Speaks Spanish	Very well	Moderate	Very well
Can create public filings	No	Yes	No
Can consolidate financial statements	No	No	Yes
Manufacturing experience	Yes	No	Yes

The preceding table forces the preparer to identify the key decision points, and makes them easier to compare across all alternatives.

Consider Hybrid Choices

It is possible that the best features of several options can be combined. To see if this is the case, go through a deliberate process of comparing and combining the features of each decision option, to see of a hybrid version is possible.

Eliminate Alternatives

At some point, it will be necessary to winnow down the number of choices from which a final selection will be made. One way to do this is the one-on-one comparison, which is the same as a playoff in sports. Under this approach, you compare how well a pair of alternatives fulfill a set of objectives. The basic rule is that, if Alternative A is better than Alternative B for some objectives and no worse than Alternative B on all other objectives, then you can eliminate Alternative B. This approach is useful for eliminating the least likely alternatives, so that you can concentrate your attention on the few remaining choices that are more complex.

EXAMPLE

Becky wants to travel from Miami to Seattle. She wants to travel in an aisle seat, pay no more than $300, and fly as close to noon as possible. Of her two best options, both cost less than $300, and depart Miami within 20 minutes of each other. However, one airline can only offer her a middle seat. Based on how well these options fulfill her objectives, she drops the option that only offers a middle seat.

Tip: When conducting this comparison, eliminate from consideration any objectives that are fulfilled equally by both alternatives. Doing so focuses your attention on the remaining objectives for which there are fulfillment differences.

In a few cases, this elimination system only leaves one remaining alternative, in which case your decision has been made.

Step 4: Make Your Choice

Based on the preceding decision steps, make your selection. In cases where there are ethical considerations, the choice made should reflect what you really care about, rather than just an interest in improving profits. After all, you will have to live with the decision. When the choice is a difficult one, give increased weight to ethical considerations. Imagine explaining your actions to a close friend – would he or she approve? If not, what sort of reaction might you expect? Several additional thoughts on making your choice appear in the following sub-sections.

Decide How to Decide

Some decisions are not obvious, so there is a tendency to wait – and wait – and wait – until more information is available from which a decision can *finally* be made. Waiting to collect more data is sensible in some situations, but can harm the business in others. When dithering over a decision, it can be useful to consider the importance and urgency of the outcome. A truly important decision (and there are not many of them) are worthy of lengthy consideration, but most decisions are nowhere near as critical to the company. In the latter case, it makes more sense to get it over with and make a decision based on the available information. Doing so allows you to reallocate your time to other, more important decisions.

When a decision really *is* important, it probably warrants some extra time in which to reflect on the available alternatives. The type of reflection time will depend on the person – perhaps sleeping on the decision, going for a walk, taking a bath, or maybe an exercise session will clear the mind to focus on the essential elements of a decision. No matter what the approach may be, it should not require more than an extra day to come to a decision.

Making use of a short delay makes it easier to avoid being influenced by emotions, such as anger that a competitor has hired away a key employee or bought a key supplier. Further, waiting allows for the collection of more evidence, the formulation of additional options, and a re-evaluation of whether the proposal under consideration is even feasible.

Note: Being able to slow down is partially based on an awareness of one's bias in favor of immediate action. When this bias is present, it can be inordinately difficult to pause, take a deep breath (or three) and consider the issues further before reaching a decision.

Only when no clear decision is forthcoming does it make sense to pause and wait to collect more data. This step should not be taken lightly, since data collection can take a long time – as well as the analysis work that goes along with it. In these cases, once you have reviewed the additional analyses and viewed the possible outcomes from every possible perspective, it is time to make a decision – dithering any longer is not a good use of your time.

> **Tip:** When a decision is being made on a recurring basis, it makes sense to track the outcome each time and develop a database of what went right or wrong, since this information can be used to enhance subsequent decisions.

The Time Tradeoff

Sometimes, a decision needs to be made right now. It cannot wait a few more months to collect more data, so waiting is out of the question. In these situations, the key is to focus on the essentials of the decision. For example, there may be 10 stakeholders, but only two of them really matter – so reach a decision that satisfies those two stakeholders, and don't worry about the rest. Or, if the decision could impact a multitude of company objectives, ignore those objectives for which the decision has only a peripheral impact. Yet another possibility is that, rather than bouncing your concerns off every associate, just talk to one person – sometimes, the simple act of explaining your dilemma will yield insights into how to proceed. By narrowing your focus in this manner, you may not arrive at the absolute best outcome, but you will come up with one that is pretty good. Doing so allows you to clear this issue off your desk, stop wasting time, and move along to the next issue.

The Review of Advocate Expertise

A valid point to explore is whether the person advocating a particular approach actually has the expertise to follow through on it. In many cases, the person's expertise is not relevant to the project that will result from a decision. If so, the manager needs to decide whether the decision outcome should include switching responsibility for the associated work to a different person. In these cases, it can make sense to appoint the original advocate to an assistant role, in order to gain experience from the person who is ultimately responsible for it.

Make Sure That the Decision is Right

Most people agonize over whether they have made the right decision, but what they tend to miss is that their subsequent actions determine how well the decision turns out to be. Thus, as soon as a decision is made, you should fully commit to its implementation, thereby improving the odds that it will turn out to be the right decision. This approach mitigates the sense of nervousness associated with making a difficult call, and instead conveys a sense of empowerment, since you will continue to have some degree of control over subsequent events.

Taking this viewpoint makes it less likely that you will be burdened by an excessive amount of analysis, since the more difficult set of options from which to select might very well all be doable – you just have to pick and proceed forcefully from there. In these situations, an additional decision factor is how motivated you feel about implementing the available decision choices. If one of the options gets you more charged up, then that may be the alternative to pursue.

> **Tip:** Explain to your subordinates your thinking about why you chose this alternative, and how their concerns were taken into account. The intent is to show that the decision-making process was fair.

Issue the Bad News

For some people, a decision will involve bad news. Perhaps they will lose their jobs, be demoted, or shifted to less interesting work. When this is the case, do not ignore or underestimate the damage. Recognize the sacrifices that some people will be making, and talk to them about it – in person. Where it is possible to do so, take steps to mitigate the negative effects of the decision on these people. For example, put them first in line for the next available promotion, to show that you are trying to be fair. Or, continue to pay people who are going to be laid off for well past their termination dates. Sidestepping this issue merely makes you look weak with your subordinates.

EXAMPLE

Colossal Furniture has completely run out of production capacity for its line of extra-wide seats, so the CEO decides to seriously delay a number of orders. Since the sales staff was going to earn significant commissions on these orders, he decides to pay their commissions anyways – even if the customers decide to cancel their orders.

Revisit the Decision

Despite the many suggestions already made in this book to improve your decision-making processes, it is still entirely possible that your ultimate choice turns out to not work very well. Assuming that this could be the case, continue to revisit the decision at frequent intervals over the first few days and weeks. By doing so, you can spot early signs that the decision is not working out. This may result in the application of more resources or the decision to switch to another option. In short, it is easiest to be aware of a looming failure as early as possible, before you become too locked into supporting it.

EXAMPLE

A chief financial officer has reviewed a number of candidates for the controller position and made his selection. The new controller has massive technical skills, but the offsetting risk is not a great deal of experience in the controller role. To see if his decision was the right one, the CFO checks in with several senior staff in the accounting department on a regular basis, and soon learns that the controller has significant weaknesses in her ability to manage others. With this information in hand, the CFO can decide whether to invest in training the controller or go in search of a replacement.

> **Tip:** Whenever you have to roll back a decision, try to extract a lesson from it, to improve the odds of making a more successful decision the next time. Perhaps this might have involved more detailed vetting of job candidates in the preceding example, or perhaps you can recognize a hiring bias, and be watchful for it in the future.

Though it may sometimes make sense to backtrack on a decision, do not follow this path too frequently. Repeated backtracking can result in an indecisive culture, where employees come to expect that decisions will be overturned. Furthermore, backtracking can negatively impact employee perceptions of you as a leader.

Conduct Milestone Reviews

A variation on the preceding point is to conduct relatively frequent milestone reviews to ensure that the implementation is following the spirit of the original decision. It is possible that some people who disagreed with the decision are attempting to warp the final outcome by making changes to the implementation plan. A continuing series of milestone reviews can spot these issues.

Conduct a Post-Project Analysis

Once a decision has been made and its ramifications have played out, set aside time to identify what went well and what went badly. This analysis can include a review of the data sources that were called upon, the data sources that were *not* called upon but which would have impacted the decision, and why one source was used but not the other. Any biases that may have skewed the decision should also be examined. By conducting this (admittedly hard) analysis, you can learn about how to improve the decision-making process the next time around.

> **Tip:** It can make sense to hire a coach, who can assist in these post-decision analyses. They can be especially good at exploring the more difficult areas that a manager might tend to avoid.

Real Options

A specialized area of decision-making is the *real option*, which refers to the decision options available for a tangible asset. The concept can be used to examine a whole range of outcomes related to an investment. For example, a traditional investment analysis in an oil refinery might use a single price per barrel of oil for the entire investment period, whereas the actual price of oil will likely fluctuate far outside of the initial estimated price point over the course of the investment, and will also vary among the different products that the refinery can manufacture. An analysis based on real options would instead focus on the range of profits and losses that may be encountered over the course of the investment period as the prices of oil and petroleum products change over time. This analysis might lead the manager of an oil refinery to repeatedly switch production among different octane grades of gasoline, to take advantage of variations in market prices. These decision points will alter the cash flows of a project.

A comprehensive real options analysis begins with a review of the risks to which a project will be subjected, and then models for each of these risks or combinations of risks. To continue with the preceding example, an investor in an oil refinery project could expand the scope of the analysis beyond the price of oil, to also encompass the risks of possible new environmental regulations on the facility, the possible downtime caused by a supply shutdown, and the risk of damage caused by a hurricane.

A logical outcome of real options analysis is to be more careful in placing large bets on a single likelihood of probability. Instead, it can make more sense to place a series of small bets on different outcomes, and then alter the portfolio of investments over time as more information about the various risks becomes available. Once the key risks have been resolved, the best investment is easier to discern, so that a "bet the bank" investment can be made. In essence, a series of small investments are made in the near future, which are the price paid in order to obtain better information concerning a larger investment to be made at a later date.

EXAMPLE

An agriculture company wants to develop a new crop strain for either wheat or barley, to be sold for export. The primary intended market is an area in which wheat is currently the preferred crop. The company estimates that it can generate a 20% return on investment by developing a new wheat variant at a cost of $30 million. Since wheat is already the primary type of crop being planted, the odds of success are high. However, if the company can successfully develop a barley variant at a total cost of $50 million, its projected profits are 50%. The key risk with the barley project is farmer acceptance. Given the high profits that could be derived from selling barley, the company makes a small initial $1 million investment in a pilot project. If the level of farmer acceptance appears reasonable, the company can then invest an additional $8 million for a further roll out of the concept, followed by additional expenditures for more extended rollouts.

This use of real options allows the company to invest a relatively small amount to test its assumptions regarding a possible alternative investment. If the test does not work, the company has only lost $1 million. If the test succeeds, the company can pursue an alternative that may ultimately yield far higher profits than the more assured investment in wheat.

The concept illustrated in the preceding example of placing a series of targeted bets can be expanded over an entire product life cycle. For example, if the pilot test for the barley variant works, the company could continue to develop options for the rollout of the product to farmers in other countries. The company may have identified certain parts of the world where cultural differences make it more or less likely that farmers will convert their fields to barley production. Accordingly, the company can invest in a target area in each of these geographic regions to measure acceptance levels, and then either proceed with a full-scale product rollout or withdraw from the market entirely. The following graphic illustrates how the process might work.

Real Options Rollout Plan for Barley Product

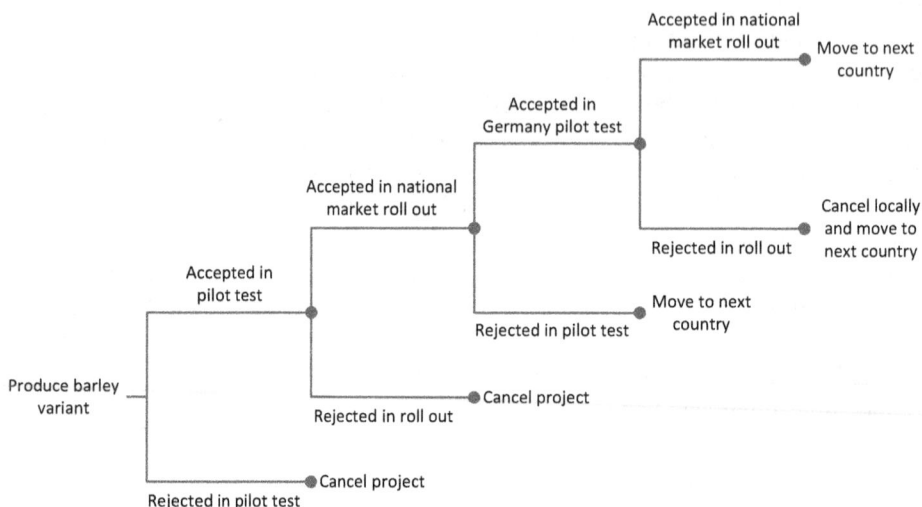

The options concept can also be used to delay a project. For example, if there is a downturn in demand or in unit prices, it can make sense to stop investing in new production capacity until market conditions are more favorable. In this case, a business is using its investment-to-date as the cost of an option that allows it to jump back into the market on short notice if conditions improve. Similarly, a real estate investor could purchase an option to buy property at a specific price and over a designated period of time. If the value of the property increases, the investor exercises the option and buys the property, earning a profit on the increase in value. If the property value does not increase, the investor lets the option expire.

Options analysis can also be used to structure the manner in which a business enters into a new market. For example, if there is uncertainty about the level of demand that will exist for a new product, a pilot plant might be constructed that is designed to have a relatively short useful life. By doing so, the investment in the new market is minimized, and the facility can be disassembled and its components sold off if demand does not materialize.

A concern with using real options is that competitors may be using the same concept at the same time, and may use the placing of small bets to arrive at the same conclusions as the company. The result can be that several competitors will enter a market at approximately the same time, driving down the initially rich margins that management may have assumed were associated with a real option. Thus, the parameters of real options constantly change, and so must be re-evaluated at regular intervals.

Another concern relates to the last point that competitors may jump into the same market. This means that a business cannot evaluate the results of its options analyses in a leisurely manner. Instead, each option must be evaluated quickly and decisions made to make additional investments (or not) before the competition gets a jump on the situation.

> **Tip:** Do not use real options merely to defer a decision. The point is to collect relevant information from these investments that will actually enhance the quality of the final decision.

> **Tip:** When deferring a decision, clearly state the date on which the issue will be revisited. Otherwise, the decision may be put off for an excessively long period of time, or may never be addressed at all.

The Qualities of Judgment

How does one manager consistently make better decisions? Some people ascribe it to a "gut feeling," which is probably based on a great deal of experience making similar decisions in the past. In these cases, the person has likely dealt with a similar issue before, and so can extract the lessons learned from that experience and subconsciously apply them to the current situation.

There are several bases upon which judgments are made. One basis is the personal qualities of the individual. These qualities include the ability to listen deeply, so that they can extract the maximum amount of information from the people involved in a decision, allowing for better insights into a solution. They rarely pontificate; instead, they give each person they are meeting their undivided attention, so that they can absorb as much information as possible from each one. To do so, they ask questions constantly, in order to draw out interesting perspectives on every possible situation. In addition, they observe the body language of the other party to see if there is additional information to be gleaned – or which might contradict what they are being told verbally.

Another personal quality is having a solid understanding of their own biases, so that they can remove these concerns from their decisions. This can be quite difficult. The decision-maker must be able to detach, both intellectually and emotionally, from the decisions being made.

EXAMPLE

When making decisions, a manager has historically only sought out information that confirms his existing opinions (confirmation bias). After being advised of this during a difficult review meeting with his boss, he begins to seek out alternative viewpoints on the decisions to be made.

One of the most difficult biases to recognize is one's inclination to do nothing. That is, most people have a bias in favor of maintaining the status quo. After all, if it has worked for us before, why change now? Even in cases where it is not especially difficult to make a change, most of us display a strong disinclination to act. By not acting, we also avoid the responsibility that accompanies making a change – which can be a significant issue in companies where people are punished for taking actions that have a poor outcome.

EXAMPLE

A senior manager with vast amounts of experience inherits a large amount of securities from his parents. These securities were issued by several highly-conservative utilities, none of which the manager would have bought on her own. Nonetheless, and despite the ease with which she could have sold the securities, she retains them for years. The status quo strikes again.

High-grade decision-makers enjoy figuring out additional solutions, which gives them a broad range of choices from which to make a selection. Some of these decisions might initially appear to be non-decisions, such as waiting to collect more information or conducting a pilot program (which is essentially also the collection of more information); in these cases, the decision-maker has concluded that a richer data set is needed to arrive at the correct conclusion, so the delay is warranted. It can also be useful to expand into the discussion of riskier options, if only to explore the cost-benefit associated with each one. In some cases, the payoff from a risky alternative could make it quite a viable alternative.

The best decision-makers are more likely to be heavily networked. That way, even if they cannot devise the best decision, they know someone who can. The best people to call upon are those who have different skill sets and experiences, so that they don't simply echo the views of the decision-maker. Instead, they have a different viewpoint on the situation, based on their backgrounds, and so can provide a different perspective on the decision to be made. The absolute best decision-makers take this networking concept to an extreme, making it a requirement for their subordinates to offer alternative viewpoints on every key decision being made. Of course, this also means that staff meetings can be unusually robust, with lots of opinions flying around the room.

EXAMPLE

The owner of a chain of retail stores is pondering opening stores for the first time in South Africa. He does not believe that his own extensive experience with operating a retail chain in the United States is relevant to the South African market, so he fosters contacts with retailing consultants in that specific market, to learn more about its pitfalls.

Another advantage of plumbing the depths of one's network is to gain a variety of viewpoints on how to proceed, which can break you free of the anchoring problem described earlier. By consulting with multiple people, it is more likely that someone will devise an outcome that falls outside of the mainstream opinions about what can be done.

Tip: When consulting with others, do not tell them too much about your own ideas, since this tends to anchor their thinking around those ideas. Instead, just give them the facts and ask them what they would do.

Another characteristic of a good decision-maker is having the relevant knowledge and experience to deal with the issue at hand. This does not mean simple book-learning – instead, it involves having a deep understanding of the underlying processes, so that they can recognize related situations that others may have missed. This knowledge of processes also allows a decision-maker to think through how difficult it would be to implement every possible outcome – which is beyond the range of someone who only has a general knowledge of the issues at hand.

> **Tip:** The best decision-makers have sought out postings in multiple functional areas, such as sales, production, and finance, so that they have a better range of knowledge from which to make decisions.

To have this level of knowledge, the best decision-makers read deeply in the topics associated with their areas of responsibility, and routinely ponder how this information can be applied to them.

> **Tip:** Senior managers rarely have time to delve into hundreds of pages of briefing materials, so they don't – instead, they insist on being provided with a cogent synopsis of each decision item, thereby keeping them from wasting time on excessive levels of detail.

Someone who routinely peruses data sources also develops the skill of questioning the information found. If the information is not well supported or does not correlate well with other information sources, the discerning manager will not accept it right away – a healthy dose of skepticism is needed to explore the information further.

The best decision-makers think about the sources of the information that they are being given. Depending on the source, it is entirely possible that the information has not been thoroughly examined for errors, or that the data collection process itself is faulty.

Special Decision Topics

In the following sub-sections, we include several additional topics relating to decision-making, including how to achieve better consistency in decision outcomes, being more efficient in making decisions, and including the concept in employee evaluations.

Decision-Making Consistency

We have included several dozen suggestions in the preceding pages for how to make better decisions. The trouble is that a person might only remember to use a few of them and even then, only on a sporadic basis. A better approach is to develop a list of action items to take for certain types of decisions, and rigidly follow these lists every time a similar decision is being made. For example, one list might be used when deciding whether to expand a product line, while another list is used to decide whether to invest in a target company. The intent is not to be overly bureaucratic, but rather to ensure that basic steps are taken during the decision-making process.

Decision-Making Efficiency

An effective manager is constantly trying to systematize the decision-making process by developing rules for how to deal with certain recurring situations where there is a low risk of failure. For example, it may be necessary to reorder inventory items on a regular basis, or buy ad space on a website, or review candidates for a position that is needed on a recurring basis. Once these situations have arisen more than once, the manager can specify how the associated decision is to be made, document these rules, and then hand off the decision to a subordinate. By taking this approach, the manager is creating more time for major, one-time decisions that are poorly defined and which have major consequences for the business – in short, decisions that require the close attention of a manager.

EXAMPLE

The manager of Optimistic Winery is faced with two decisions – which supplier to use for the company's annual purchase of wine bottles, and how wide the row width should be for ten new acres of vine plantings in the south fields. Though the bottle purchase is a large one, it can be safely left in the hands of the purchasing manager, since it is a repetitive inventory purchase. The row width decision, however, is much more important, since it impacts the amount of grapes that can be produced and the types of tractors that can be used in the vineyard – and the decision cannot be reversed until the field is replanted in 30 years. Thus, the manager can hand off the bottle purchase decision, so that she can focus more of her time on the row width decision.

Decision Advocacy Targeting

Throughout this book, we have targeted the right way to engage in decision-making. It is also useful to describe the *wrong* approach, in which different camps within the business heavily advocate their own viewpoints regarding which alternative should be selected. The characteristics of an advocacy environment are when decision-making is treated more as a contest to see who wins than a mutual exploration of the available options. Advocacy also involves heavy lobbying of the decision-maker and his or her close associates, where the weaknesses of a particular alternative are downplayed and the attractiveness of its best features are overblown. In this environment, minority views are much more likely to be squashed or dismissed out of hand. And, once a decision has been made, there is a winning camp and a losing camp – with the latter group resenting the outcome and quite possibly trying to undermine it.

The advocacy approach is obviously detrimental to the development of good decisions, so when employees present the advocacy characteristics, it is time to restructure the process. Ideally, it should emphasize a collective evaluation of options, using constructive criticism of every option in order to arrive at an outcome of which everyone can take collective ownership.

Negotiations

Anchoring is a particular concern when you are engaged in negotiations. When the other party makes an initial offer, it is quite likely that subsequent negotiations will center around that offer. The first step in avoiding anchoring is to understand its presence. That allows you to set boundaries well away from the other party's offer.

The anchoring concept can also be used to your advantage. Lead with your proposal, using a price point that is high yet defensible, so that the negotiations proceed from that point. By doing so, the final terms are more likely to be in your favor.

Employee Retention

When a business is in difficult financial condition, one of the more difficult decisions for managers is which people need to be laid off. Sometimes, this decision is based entirely on how much they cost the company in terms of their compensation and benefits. What this analysis misses is that employees with more time on the job tend to make better decisions. Because these people have repetitively dealt with numerous situations and (hopefully) learned from their mistakes, they are more likely to make better decisions when confronted with these situations again. So, when deciding who has to leave the company during a downturn, keep in mind that the more experienced people can keep your company from making some serious mistakes.

That being said, it is less necessary to retain more experienced employees when the problems people are dealing with mostly have clear decision rules, objective criteria, and lots of data available on which to perform an analysis. In these cases, decisions are more clear-cut and require less judgment.

Performance Evaluations

When evaluating employee performance, it can be useful to review the quality of their decision-making, with due consideration of the information that was available to them at the time. By doing so, even if the decisions made turn out to be incorrect, you can gain a better understanding of how they are likely to deal with difficult decisions in the future.

A related part of this analysis is to also review whether a person merely benefited from lucky circumstances, such as entering a market at the exact time when customer demand took off, or a competitor went bankrupt. These events may have masked a poor underlying decision-making process, for which the person should be penalized.

Summary

It can be quite difficult to develop high-quality business decisions. The average person's decision-making processes are riddled with shortcuts, biases, and misperceptions that routinely result in sub-optimal decisions. However, being aware of the concepts described in this book can at least make you aware of these concerns, if not reduce them to more manageable levels. In particular, we recommend that you develop a set of decision checklists to follow for each type of major decision, so that decisions can be made in as consistent a manner as possible.

Glossary

A

Anchoring. The tendency to rely too heavily on one piece of information when making decisions.

B

Brainstorming. A process used to generate ideas by engaging in an open group discussion.

C

Confirmation bias. When the decision-maker only seeks out others who have the same opinions.

G

Groupthink. When the need for conformity results in a dysfunctional decision-making outcome.

M

Murphy's Law. The adage that anything that can go wrong, will go wrong.

R

Root cause analysis. The process of looking for the reasons why a problem is occurring.

S

Sunk cost. A cost that has been incurred and which can no longer be recovered.

Index

www.ingramcontent.com/pod-product-compliance
Lightning Source LLC
Chambersburg PA
CBHW051430200326
41520CB00023B/7416